LILLIAN TOO'S
FENG SHUI
IN SMALL DOSES

for
WORK & CAREER

Feng shui in small doses for
Work & Career.
by
Lillian Too
© Konsep Lagenda S/B

ISBN 983 - 9778 - 13 - 7

Lillian Too's feng shui in small doses

Also in this series

Wealth
and Prosperity

Romance, Love &
Marriage

Published by
KONSEP BOOKS
Malaysia
April 2000

For Work & Career

www.wofs.com

*For
all kind of
feng shui freebies*

1

I hold an MBA from the
Harvard Business School
which helped open many
career opportunities for
me. But my knowledge of
feng shui gave me an extra
edge in negotiations,
gaining recognition, and
winning promotions.

2

The universal career corner applicable for everyone is the north corner of the office or living room. If this corner is properly activated with moving water, it creates excellent career luck for the residents.

3

The trigram for the north is KAN, which represents a situation of entanglement and perpetual danger. It indicates that career people should always have the north sector guarded so they do not suffer unhappiness due to office politics & intrigues.

4

All ambitious career people
should protect their careers
and their career luck by
either having real tortoises
(or terrapins) swimming
happily in a pond or an
aquarium in the north or at
least have the image of the
turtle here.

5

Another excellent idea is to keep a pet terrapin in your office. Keep him on a table or cupboard behind you. This ensures that precious turtle energy, which gives continuing protection from office politics, will always be there for you.

6

Take note that you must never overdo the presence of water. Too much water will drown you. So size of aquariums should not overwhelm your office. This could cause you to get fired ! In the use of water. less is always better.

7

Protect the north corner by applying the principles of the five elements. Water is produced by metal, so metal windchimes, computers and other metallic equipment brings good career luck when placed in the north.

8

The north sector of both your home and office will benefit from the placement of a water feature since north belongs to the water element. Installing a mini fountain, an aquarium or a even a small pond in the north brings excellent career luck.

9

Water produces wood, so wood exhausts water. This means that anything made of wood or symbolizing wood placed in the north will exhaust your career luck. So avoid having decorative plants and flowers in the north sectors of office or desk.

10

Water is destroyed by earth, so anything made of, or symbolizing earth could cause setbacks in your career luck. Do not place crystals, ceramic objects or other clay or porcelain objects in the north. Amazingly yes, they hurt your career.

11

Calculate your KUA number to find out your most favourable compass orientations at work. This Eight Mansions feng shui formula uses your Chinese year of birth and gender to work out your personal KUA formula.

12

Each person has a KUA
number which indicates the
career success direction.
This is your sheng chi

KUA #	SHENG CHI
1	Southeast
2	Northeast
3	South
4	North
5 male	Northeast
5 female	Southwest
6	West
7	Northwest
8	South
9	East

13

Your KUA number is calculated from your Chinese year of birth. Those born before the lunar New Year or before Feb 4th should deduct one year from their year of birth to get the equivalent Chinese year. Those born after the New Year or after the 4th Feb. need not make any adjustments.

14

Add the last two digits of the year of birth until you obtain a single digit. Then deduct this from 10 for males; and add 5 for females. Thus if date of birth is 5ᵗʰ March 1944. Add last two digits 4 + 4=8. For men 10 – 8 = 2 so KUA is 2. For women 5 + 8=13 and then 1+3=4. Kua number is 4.

15

Commit your sheng chi
direction to memory since
this success direction has
many different uses.

You can use it when at
negotiations, at meetings,
during presentations and to
arrange the feng shui of
your personal sitting space
at work.

16

Use your personal sheng chi direction to select your office. If you have a choice of offices, invest in a compass to find out which part of the office corresponds to your sheng chi. Then try to locate your office there.

17

If you cannot get the sheng chi location for your office, try to have the entrance door into your office facing your sheng chi direction. This brings enormous success luck. Direction is always taken inside facing outwards.

18

Next, position your office desk in such a way that when you sit, you are able to face your sheng chi direction. Use a black marker pen and mark this direction with an arrow so you never forget.

19

Unless there are other feng shui reasons not to do so, always face your sheng chi direction each time you have a discussion with someone at your office and when you are engaged in an important phone conversation.

20

Observe this same rule
when making an important
presentation, conducting a
seminar or making a sales
pitch – always face your
sheng chi. Carry a pocket
compass to quickly check
your orientations.
This tip always works !

21

At management and budget meetings always sit facing your sheng chi direction. Since this is when you are "on show" so to speak, never compromise on your directions. Go early to get the seat you want but don't be obvious about it !

22

If it is impossible to tap your sheng chi direction use one of the other three lucky directions, which belong to the same group of directions as your sheng chi. This ensures you will not be facing one of your four unlucky directions.

23

The lucky directions of East & West group KUA numbers are shown here.

EAST GROUP	WEST GROUP
Kua numbers are 1, 3, 4 and 9	Kua numbers are 2, 5, 6, 7, and 8
Lucky directions are East, SE, North and South	Lucky directions are West, SW, NE and NW

24

Energizing the metal element in the North is an excellent way of enhancing career luck and this gets multiplied when the Northwest is also similarly activated with metal. The Northwest is crucial for ambitious career types

25

Hang a 6 rod hollow
metal windchime to
energize the northwest.
This activates mentor
luck. The more happily
your windchime tinkles
and moves, the more
your career will benefit
from support of
powerful mentors.

26

I used to hang a large
windchime in my office
and to make sure it tinkled
continuously I placed a
stand fan blowing at it all
day long. My metal
element chi flowed
powerful and strong …
and my career took off !

27

The Northwest corner
of your office is also the
perfect place to put your
computer. Moving images
and constant use of the
computer creates precious
yang energy here. The
Northwest benefits the
most from yang chi.

28

Another very lucky symbol
perfect for activating
auspicious chi in the
northwest corner of your
office is the horseshoe.
Magnets that have this
shape attract strong,
powerful and beneficial
patrons who will help you
in your career.

29

Special bells, cast from seven types of metals (including gold and silver), symbolize high positions. If you are after a promotion or in the running for an important job, having this bell in the North or Northwest will enhance your chances.

30

In the old days Chinese court officials wore embroidered insignias of auspicious symbols on their chests, to signify their high rank. The equivalent of these auspicious power symbols would be ties for men and scarves for women; and good fortune jewellery for both.

31

Look for ties, tiepins and cufflinks that feature auspicious symbols. For career luck, the best symbol is the celestial dragon. Choose discreet designs and prints. Wearing dragons or any celestial symbol in an overpowering fashion can cause imbalance.

32

Other significant and powerful symbols which can be activated for upward mobility luck in your career are the legendary unicorn, the chi lin, and the celestial phoenix. Wear these symbols to generate their heavenly chi.

33

The phoenix always brings opportunities. This is the creature you absolutely must activate when you are down, unemployed and jobless. The phoenix is an exceptionally good symbol to help you when you are down. Hang a painting of the phoenix.

34

The chi lin and unicorn are legendary for their protective chi. I recommend them over the tiger because they never turn on you. Place a small pair on the two outer edges of your desk or table to guard against being a victim of office intrigues.

35

Career luck can turn sour if your sitting position is afflicted. Look up to check if anything threatening is hanging above your head. Do not sit under a wooden or structural beam, or an air conditioner.
Move your desk from under these things.

36

Ceiling lines and sharp
design patterns can create
slivers of killing energy in
the same way beams do.

Either move your sitting
location or shine a light
upwards at the lines to
dissolve any bad energy
created.

37

Sitting directly under a
ceiling fan creates
turbulence in the air above
you. This is not good for
your career luck.
Move out of the direct
blast of fast moving air.
The chi of such air
is afflicted.

38

It is a bad idea to have exposed open shelves behind you or in front of you at work. They signify knives sending cutting chi into you. Exposed shelves cause serious illness, loss of income as well as loss of influence and authority. Either close with doors or remove them altogether.

39

Never ever sit with a door
behind you especially if it
is the entrance door into
your office. This will cause
you to get "stabbed in the
back". Employees will
cheat you. Colleagues will
badmouth you and bosses
will dump you.

40

Watch what you place on
your desk. Avoid objects
that are sharp and with
edges pointed directly at
you. Also avoid placing the
image of wild animals like
the tiger, the leopard and
the lion on your desk,
especially facing you.

41

Never allow files to get
piled high on your desk
directly in front of you.
These signify a mountain
blocking your chi.
Your ambitions will
similarly get blocked.
Files piled high behind
and to the sides of your
desk are fine.

42

It is a good idea to energize your desk with good fortune symbols. Place them according to the compass sector of your desk. Draw an imaginary Lo Shu square on the desk and use a compass to determine their directions.

43

If possible place a bright
lamp in the South corner
of your desk. This will
activate your recognition
luck, and ensure that you
will get noticed by a
person of influence who
can help you. Keep the
light turned on.

44

Always place fresh
flowers them on the east,
southeast or south corners
of the desk.
This stimulates the growth
chi of the wood element.
It ensures steady and
positive development of
your career.

45

Place computers, telephones and calculators in the west or NW corner of your desk. This activates their metal element. When the NW is successfully energized you will receive favourable attention from your bosses.

46

To ensure that news which comes to you via telephone, email or fax is more good news than bad, try to position these machines in such a way that the energy gets plugged in from your sheng chi direction.

47

You can stick an auspicious
symbol on your telephone
to create the chi of
successful phone
conversations. This is
excellent for those who do
the bulk of their job
through the telephone.
Example: Stick three coins
tied together with red
thread on your telephone.

48

My mobile phones, note books and even my handbags are always strongly energized with small images of my favourite symbols – that of coins, toads or dragons. I find these images in different parts of the world at flea markets and bazaars.

49

Every office has its own "lucky location" and if you have your desk here, your personal workspace is benefiting from the divine natural chi of good fortune. According to From School feng shui the best corner is the corner diagonally opposite to the main door.

50

You can use flying star
feng shui to locate the most
auspicious corner of any
office building.

To do this you need to
know when the building
was built and you need to
determine its exact front
entrance orientation.

51

A period 7 office building that facing South 1 ie between 157.5 to 172,5 degrees has three auspicious corners, at the back of the building in the north and northeast sectors, and in the front south sector. The entrance of this building is also auspicious.

52

A period 7 office building which faces South 2/3 (between 172.5 to 202,5 degrees) has two lucky sectors in the front, in the south and southwest corners as well as one at the back in the north corner of the building.

53

A period 7 building facing
North 1 (between 337.5 to
352,5 degrees) has two
auspicious corners in the
front of the building in the
north and northeast sectors
and one lucky sector at the
back in the south. Placing a
waterfall directly in front
of the building brings
money luck to tenants.

54

A period 7 building that
faces North 2/3 (between
352.5 to 022,5 degrees)
has two auspicious corners
at the back of the building
in the south and SW
building. The entrance
north grid is also lucky.
Water in the SW corner of
any office in such a
building benefits
occupants' success luck.

55

A period 7 office building facing the direction of West 1 (between 247.5 to 262.5 degrees) has one lucky location in front in the NW corner and one lucky corner at the back in the SE corner.
Both these corners will benefit from a water feature.

56

A period 7 building facing West 2/3 (between 262.5 to 292 degrees) has two lucky sectors in front of the building in the west and northwest sectors, and one lucky corner at the back in the SE corner. A water feature in the SE or NW brings financial success.

57

A period 7 building facing
East 1(between 067.5 to
082.5 degrees) has one
lucky sector in front in the
East where the main door
is located and one lucky
sector at the back in the
NW corner of the building.
The auspicious water star
is in your NE corner.

58

A period 7 building
facing East 2/3 (between
082.5 to 112.5 degrees)
has its lucky sectors
located in the SE and
West of the building.

The lucky water star is in
the SW corner of offices.

59

A period 7 building
facing Southwest 1
(between 202.5 to 217.5
degrees) has lucky sectors
in the SW in front of the
building and in the back
sectors North and East.
Water in the north of the
building or offices creates
enormous money luck.

60

A period 7 building that
faces Southwest 2/3
(between 217.5 to 247.5
degrees) enjoys plenty of
money luck. The lucky
sectors are the South and
West at the front of the
building and NE behind.
Water placed in front of
the building enhances the
luck of the building.

61

A period 7 building facing Southeast 1 (between 112.5 to 127.5 degrees) has its lucky sector in the center of the building. Offices located in the center have the best luck. Activate your own luck by having a goldfish bowl on the east corner of your desk or office.

For Work & Career

62

A period 7 building facing Southeast 2/3 (between 127.5 to 157.5 degrees) has its most auspicious location in the center of the building... if your office is inside such a building, energize good luck by placing water in the west corner of your personal office.

63

A period 7 building facing Northeast 1 (between 022.5 to 037.5 degrees) has two lucky sectors in the front of the building, at the North and east corners, plus one lucky sector in the SW grid at the back of the building. Individual offices can be made extremely lucky by energizing the East corner.

64

A period 7 building facing
Northeast 2/3 (between
037.5 to 0675 degrees) has
a lucky main door. The
lucky locations of the
building are at the back in
the west and south corners.
Water features placed in
the west bring money luck.

65

A period of 7 building
facing Northwest
1(between 292.5 to 307.5
degrees) has a lucky central
grid. The East also has
some lucky stars. Offices
with such a building should
energize with the picture of
a mountain range or a
dragon in their east corner.

66

A period 7 building facing Northwest 2/3 (between 307.5 to 337.5 degrees) also has a very lucky central grid. Offices here enjoy excellent feng shui. The west corner of this building is very lucky. Private offices will benefit from placing a mountain picture in the west.

67

A period 7 building is a
building that is constructed
or renovated during the
period of 7 ie between Feb
4th 1984 to Feb 4th 2004.
The next twenty-year
period is the period of 8.
Buildings that are
renovated in the next
period will need to re
evaluate their feng shui.

68

The "power place" for
your desk is always
diagonal to the door.
So endeavour to sit in the
corner furthest from the
door and looking at the
door. It is only after you
have done this that you
orientate your desk to face
your sheng chi.

69

If there are two people sitting in the room, try not to sit directly facing each other as this is deemed to be confrontational and will create the bull fighting killing chi which results in quarrels and misunderstandings.

70

Do not have the edge of a
pillar directly pointed at
you. This will cause you to
get ill. You could also
become the victim of
gossip and innuendoes in
the office. A plant will
dissolve the killing energy.
Change the plant every
three months.

71

Always have a solid wall,
a screen or a divider
behind you.
This will give you support,
and also ensures that no
one sabotages your work.
For double strength
hang a picture of a big
mountain behind you.

72

Another excellent career tip is to place a ceramic turtle, hang a picture of a turtle or place real terrapins behind you.

This symbolizes the protective chi of this celestial creature. He also ensures longevity of tenure at your job.

73

A powerful feng shui energizer for enhanced career luck is the image of a successful person you admire. Place a picture of your role model in the NW (if he is male) or SW (if she is female) at your office to create the chi of your success expectations.

74

Never place your desk too
excessively near the door
since the chi that enters
will cause you more harm
than good. This bad
arrangement will be
compounded if your door is
afflicted in any way, either
because of being too near a
toilet or facing a
straight corridor.

75

You should try to avoid sitting in a triangular shape room since this means your career will be short-lived.

If you have no choice, try to regularize the shape of the room with clever furniture arrangement.

76

Big wall mirrors can be used to regularize the shape of an unbalanced office. Mirrors are also good for creating a sense of space when the office seems too cramped. But for mirrors to work, they should not reflect corners or doors.

77

Avoid working in a room
that has a sloping ceiling.
If you have no choice, then
sit under where the ceiling
is higher and place a
standing light to shine up at
the ceiling where it is
sloping down. Place green
plants here to counter.

78

Do not to sit with your back to the window since this symbolizes a lack of support. Your ideas and suggestions will have no support from colleagues and bosses. Change your sitting orientation (even if it is your sheng chi direction) or cover the window with solid blinds.

79

If there is a solid building
outside your window and
especially if it is a
building, which houses an
important Govt. agency or
a bank, then it is perfectly
fine to have the window
behind you. Keep the
window open since this
means you have
good support.

80

You should never occupy
an office that is situated at
the end of a long straight
corridor. The chi, which
hits your door and office,
contains killing energy.
Place a screen just
inside your office to
slow it down.

81

Your feng shui at work is better if the way to your desk follows a meandering rather than a straight path.

So try to create an auspicious route by taking a meandering rather than a straight path to your desk.

82

During the lunar New Year there is a great method of enhancing your career luck. This tradition, passed on to me by my Cantonese associates in Hong Kong, was to be given flowers grown from bulbs e.g. hyacinths and narcissus plants. These symbolize the blossoming of career luck.

83

Another career enhancing ritual during the New Year is to display the dragon carp - a special symbol of authority, which indicates an elevation in status during the coming year. This signifies the humble carp crossing the Dragon Gate to transform into a mighty dragon.

84

The Dragon carp jumping over the Dragon gate is an excellent gift for young people who are just entering the job market after graduating from College as it signifies getting good employment with good prospects.

85

Strengthen the influence of the trigram Chien to enhance your working luck. These three solid line represents the awesome power of patronage luck. Helpful people will materialize in your life if you incorporate three solid lines into the décor of the North west corners of your desk or office.

86

Many Chinese are fond of "inviting" the Taoist God of war and wealth – Kuan Kung – into their homes and offices in the belief that this deity gives both protection and good luck to those in a competitive situation. Place Kuan Kung in the Northwest of your office or behind you.

87

An alternative are the three
Star Gods – Fuk Luk Sau
which are the deities
representing health, wealth
and happiness. These
deities are symbolic and
are not regarded as holy
objects. Place images of
them behind you at work.

88

Select your Fuk Luk Sau
according to the compass
direction of your <u>sitting</u>
position. In feng shui this
is the opposite of your
facing direction. So if you
face east, then your sitting
direction is considered to
be west. If you face NW
your sitting direction
is SE and so on.

89

If your sitting position is SW or NE a Fuk Luk Sau made of ceramic or porcelain enhances the earth element. If your sitting position is NW, North or West get a set made of cloisonné or copper. If East, South or Southeast get a set carved out of wood.

90

If you want to be
successful in your career,
you should not have
artificially stunted trees in
your office or at home.
These bonsai plants are
very bad news. They
signify a curbing of your
growth and upward
mobility.

91

Cactus and other spiky plants are also feng shui taboos. Do not have them by your office windows. Cactus causes the relationships in the office with colleagues and employees to become prickly and unfriendly.

92

Positioning your rice cooker in such a way that the electricity enters the rice cooker from your sheng chi direction can activate career success. (See Tip 12 for your sheng chi direction). Make sure the maid does not change this position.

93

You can also position the
kettle which boils all the
hot water you use in the
same way. Position it so
that the plug is pointed to
your sheng chi direction.
Note that I am referring to
the kettle plug and not to
the wall plug.

94

When dining at business
functions and office dinners
always sit facing your
sheng chi direction. Carry
a pocket compass to ensure
that you observe this as
often as possible. I used to
do this all the time when I
was working.

95

Always protect your career
luck by guarding against
being hit by the bad energy
of toilets. So don't share a
wall with a toilet on the
other side. Don't sit under
a toilet on upper floor and
don't sit directly facing a
toilet door.

96

Career luck becomes
badly afflicted if the
main door of your home
is located directly under a
toilet on the upstairs floor.

This affliction is difficult to
overcome. Try shining a
bright light upwards to
'raise the chi'.

97

Do not sit with a pillar
directly in front of you.
Also do not sit with a wall
too close, directly in front
of you. This creates
unnecessary obstacles and
slows down your career
progress significantly.
Keep some space between
your table and the wall in
front of you.

98

Never hang the picture of a mountain on the wall in front of you. This represents the blockage of chi. Instead place paintings of open fields, lakes and cultivated land with crops ready for harvest instead. Most auspicious.

99

Career luck is influenced by the way you sleep. When your bedroom is located in your sheng chi direction, and you sleep with your head (when you are lying down) pointed to sheng chi direction, success at work comes easily.

100

Getting the sheng chi
sleeping direction exactly
right is not always
possible. While it is
acceptable to position your
bed at an angle to the wall
to tap the sheng chi, you
should not do it if the angle
gets too pronounced.

101

Make it a habit to always
sleep with a solid wall
behind you. This ensures
stability and balance during
your hours of rest, and you
will have a peaceful sleep.
If there is a window
above you, close it
with curtains.

102

Don't sleep under an
exposed overhead beam.
When the beam is directly
above your head, it affects
your judgements and
decisions at work, and
when the beam is cutting
your body, you will
suffer from illness.

103

Avoid being 'hit' by the
sharp edge of a protruding
corner of your bedroom.
In the bedroom you
should not use plants to
camouflage the edge.
I suggest that you place a
piece of furniture against
the edge instead.

104

Do not place your bed between two doors especially if one is the door into the toilet. Sleeping between two doors on either side of you has a negative impact on your success luck. Use a screen to block one of the doors.

105

Always sleep on a bed,
which has a headboard as
this gives good support
when you sleep.

A rounded headboard is
better than a fancy
headboard. Brass beds do
not offer sufficient support.

106

If you have mirrors in your office try not to have them on the wall directly facing you. When you work with a big mirror directly in front of you, all your luck at work tend to get dissipated. Mirrors are acceptable only on walls on either side of you.

107

It is not conducive to good
feng shui if the foyer of
your office has a mirror
directly facing the door.
This cause good luck
entering the office to get
reflected out instantly.
Mirrors directly facing
main entrances are
always bad news.

108

Office reception areas
always benefit from being
well lighted. When this
part of the office has a
bright light benevolent and
auspicious chi enters and
benefits everyone inside the
office. If this place is dim
and dark, the energy
is not auspicious.

109

Design your calling cards according to feng shui principles. Make sure the card is well balanced and have your name in larger fonts than the title. Do not let anything sharp be pointed at your name, and place your name above the corporate name.

110

Calling cards that follow
feng shui dimensions are
luckier. Conventional
calling cards are
acceptable because one
side has lucky dimensions.
Black print on white
paper is excellent. Gray on
white is less lucky.

111

Colour combinations on calling cards that are to be avoided are red print on white paper; green on white, and black on cream. Colour combinations that are auspicious are blue or purple on white paper; red on cream paper, and gold or metallic on black.

112

Sign all your important documents with the prosperity signature. Always start and end your signature with an upward stroke. Make sure there is not even a hint of a backward or downward stroke at the end. The more times you go over your name in the signature the more energy it has !

113

Be aware of lucky and unlucky numbers. The lucky numbers are always 1, 6 and 8. These represent the luck of heaven, earth and mankind. Try to have these numbers incorporated onto your phone and car numbers.

114

The number 7 is lucky until Feb 4th 2004. The luckiest number is 8, which represents coming prosperity. The number 9 represent the fullness of heaven and earth. 9 has the power to enhance all other numbers for good or bad. So 8 followed with 9 strengthens good fortune.

115

The bad luck numbers are
5 and 2. When these
numbers appear with
the 9 then the bad
represented by the 2 and 5
are magnified. But 2 with 8
is lucky just as a double 5
can be lucky because
they add up to 10.

116

Always take note of the position of the deadly five yellow in any year and avoid sitting in this location in that year. So avoid sitting in the NORTH in 2000; in the Southwest in 2001, in the EAST in 2002 and in the SOUTHEAST IN 2003. Don't let the 5 yellow destroy your career

For Work & Career

117

Don't allow the 'three killings' to block your career path either. Note its direction each year so you never sit with your back to it. Otherwise you will get stabbed in the back. The 3 killings is in the South in 2000, in the East in 2001

118

A third orientation taboo to be aware of is that you should respect the place of the Grand Duke Jupiter. If you disturb or confront the Grand Duke's home with excessive noise, renovation or if you sit facing (confronting) it, you will lose out in the promotion stakes. You could even get axed from your job.

119

The Palace of the Grand
Duke occupies only 15
degrees of the compass.
Take note of the compass
direction occupied
by him each year.
In the next two years the
GDJ lives in East/SE in
2000 and in
South/SE in 2001

120

In 2000, those born under the animal sign of the Dog clash with the Grand Duke. Place plants in the East – southeast as a cure. In 2001 Boars need the protection of a pair of fu dogs at the entrance. In 2002 Rat year people should light up their south.

121

Career conscious people can enhance career and work luck, by placing the jade Ru-yi, an old symbol of authority in the Chinese court. Place one on your table to gain promotion to higher managerial levels

122

The dragon is an excellent symbol for attracting courageous career luck. Anyone can use or wear the dragon with confidence. There are many ways to energize the luck of the dragon. Use it as your personal emblem. Wear a dragon tie pin or a dragon brooch.

123

Place the image of a dragon on the East or Southeast corner of your office or table. Do not put a large, oversized dragon. Those without the intrinsic strength to have such a powerful symbol could get sick. Small dragon images are always safer and just as effective as large ones.

124

A powerful image which can be successfully energized is the wish fulfilling cow sitting on a bed of coins and gold ingots. Place it as decorative object on your desk for prosperous harmony.

125

Combine the awesome
power of the dragon with
the benign protective
energies of the turtle in an
image of the dragon
tortoise sitting on a bed of
coins. Use it as a
paperweight at work.

126

People whose KUA numbers are 7 should have been enjoying a run of good fortune which will not end until Feb 2004. Those with KUA numbers 5 and 8 will enjoy excellent good fortune during the twenty years of the period of 8, from year 2004 to 2024.

127

Learn to purify your personal work space. An easy way to do this is to invest in a singing bowl made from seven types of metal including gold and silver. Use a wooden mallet to create the singing sound which dissolves accumulated bad energies. Do this once a month.

128

Another easy way to clear
your work space of bad
energy created by
quarrelsome colleagues is
to burn sandalwood incense
around your office. Move
in a clockwise direction
round the room three times
with the burning incense.
Early morning time is best.

© Lillian Too

This little book is
dedicated to my family

FENG SHUI
on line at

www.worldoffengshui.com

www.lillian-too.com

www.lilliantoojewellery.com

EMAIL the author at
Feng shui@ lillian-too.com